IMAGES
of America

DUDE RANCHING IN WYOMING

On the Cover: Demonstrating his commitment to educating his guests about the West, Larry Larom, owner of Valley Ranch, is seen spending time with children talking about aspects of Western life. During the Great Depression, the numbers of boy and girl guests dwindled. Larom decided to combine the two in order to keep them going. They were finally discontinued in 1942, because wartime conditions meant a shortage of labor and rail transport. (Courtesy of American Heritage Center, University of Wyoming.)

IMAGES
of America

DUDE RANCHING IN WYOMING

Russell True and Christine Holden

ARCADIA
PUBLISHING

ISBN 978-1-4671-0333-6

Published by Arcadia Publishing
Charleston, South Carolina

Library of Congress Control Number: 2019947611

For all general information, please contact Arcadia Publishing:
Telephone 843-853-2070
Fax 843-853-0044
E-mail sales@arcadiapublishing.com
For customer service and orders:
Toll-Free 1-888-313-2665

Visit us on the Internet at www.arcadiapublishing.com

Dedicated to Mac Makenny, Sarah Stevenson, and Ken Neal,
Dude Ranchers' Association presidents and friends.

Contents

ACKNOWLEDGMENTS

Dude ranching is a small business segment that has had a far larger role in the West than anyone would ever guess. I have been fascinated by people drawn to it, both the owners and staff and the dudes. When I was first elected to the Dude Ranchers' Association board around 1995, I joined a group of veteran dude ranchers from whom I immediately began to learn. Three of those people were past, present, and future presidents of what we all call the DRA. All three, Mac Makenny, Sarah Stevenson, and Ken Neal, showed me how to think, how to run a meeting, and how to be a much better dude rancher and person. The entire board viewed modern dude ranching through the prism of its history and tradition. Through their eyes, I became fascinated with dude ranching's past.

After putting together *Dude Ranching in Arizona*, Wyoming was the natural next destination. My father was born there, and the rest of his family never left. It is the location where dude ranching took hold and grew.

My mother-in-law, Chris Holden, a lover and teacher of literature, was a huge help with the first book. I knew the Wyoming book would be a big project and asked her to coauthor it. Fortunately, she accepted, and this is our shared effort. We thank Colleen Hodson of the Dude Ranchers' Association for her extensive efforts in pushing the too-busy ranchers to contribute photographs and history and for her very wise counsel. Her input is invaluable, as she is the one person on earth who has been to all 100-plus ranches in the association. The Dude Ranch Foundation played a crucial role in providing many of the great photographs included. We can relate to how hard it is for a rancher to find the time to track down the photographs and send them in, so we especially thank them.

The book would not have been completed without Susanne Walsh and Brook Grobosky, who helped with research, photographs, writing, and layout.

INTRODUCTION

Adventure-seeking tourists—dudes—came West to see the big unspoiled country, ride horseback, hunt, fish, and experience ranch life. Many of the travelers stayed on working cattle ranches and dude ranches. These lodgings sprang up independently in various locations. Most did not last long and are lost to history. Brothers Alden, Howard, and Willis Eaton came into dude ranching reluctantly, but once convinced by a guest to accept money for his stay, they saw the natural fit of the Western experience for the dudes and the financial support it provided to the tough and precarious business of ranching.

It was generally accepted that nearly all successful dude ranches had an Eastern connection. These connections naturally led ranches to draw from specific areas. Famous people were also a draw. Theodore Roosevelt was friends with the Eatons; Buffalo Bill was associated with the town named for him, Cody; and Owen Wister, the author of *The Virginian*, was linked to the Jackson/Teton area.

With the dudes living in Eastern cities, the ranchers went to them in the winters. They visited friendly dudes who invited their friends to meet the ranchers. Much like the country clubs that many of the dudes were members of, dude ranches had exclusive guest lists. References were generally required, and certain groups were not welcome.

By 1930, there were 100-plus dude ranches in Wyoming, with 31 ranches in the Sheridan area and 21 in the Jackson area. Since many of the dude ranchers were from somewhere else, some locals viewed them as outsiders. The dudes were elites whose wealth and influence contributed to the growth of Wyoming. Some were artists and authors who brought positive attention to the state.

Dude ranching in Wyoming had grown to the point where, in 1934, the University of Wyoming began offering a degree in recreational ranching with courses in institutional management, cuisine, animal production, zoology, geology, Western lore, veterinary science, and agronomy. The diversity of the program acknowledged the wide range of skills dude ranchers needed to be successful.

Maxwell Struthers Burt of the Bar BC Ranch was one of the many young men sent West by their families to find their way. He became a successful cattleman and dude rancher. In his 1924 autobiography, *The Diary of a Dude Wrangler*, he gave the following description, which is mostly still true:

> A dude-ranch is not a summer hotel, nor is it a summer board-house, much as it may seem like one or the other to the ignorant. Physically it is an ordinary ranch amplified. In some sections of the country the buildings are made out of logs, in others out of adobe, or frame, or even brick. There is usually a large central ranch-house containing sitting rooms, a dining-room, kitchens, storehouses, and so on, and, scattered about the grounds, smaller cabins or houses, holding from one to four people, used as sleeping-quarters. There is invariably a great variety of other buildings, ice-houses, saddle-sheds, blacksmith shops, camp storehouses, frequently a store and post office and almost always

> an extra large cabin that can be used for dancing. And as a rule, unless the ranch is an old ranch turned into a dude-ranch, the dude-wrangler has picked his location for its beauty and if he is a wise dude wrangler that there is no effect of crowding or of size. You must do your best, even on a place where from fifty to over a hundred people are gathered together, not to destroy the impression of wildness and isolation.

Most ranches were small, with guest capacities of 35 to 40, which is still true today. In Wyoming, nearly all are seasonal, with summer being peak season and late spring and early fall being shoulder seasons. Today, some ranches are open in the winter for snow sports as bed-and-breakfasts.

Dude ranches have always had many challenges, several of which are unique to the industry. They are small businesses built around expansive, unspoiled, beautiful country that also supports extensive riding programs. With mostly live-on staff, horses that need to be fed and cared for, higher costs due to location and logistics, and short seasons, ranches need to stay fairly full. The positive to all these challenges is that dude ranching will remain a business only for owners and managers who believe in the unique and special experience that they share with their guests.

One

THE FIRSTS

Dude ranching is likely the West's first destination vacation. The wealthy elite from the East and Midwest took long trips on trains, stages, wagons, and horses to ranches. They stayed for months and entire summers. They came to ride the unspoiled wilderness with cowboys, experience or at least witness the cowboy life, and see and hunt the plentiful wildlife.

In the early days, it became obvious to many that successful ranches had both Western and Eastern influences. Often a Westerner teamed up with someone from the East. But Easterners also came out West and learned the practical realities of stock raising and harsh, remote living, then turned to their connections to and understanding of the populated East to bring dudes to their ranches.

Two firsts in dude ranching were in Wyoming. The first dude ranch was the Eatons', and the first president of the Dude Ranchers' Association was Larry Larom of the Valley Ranch. Both were perfect examples of the power of the East as dude ranching began.

The Eatons likely changed American history indirectly by writing a letter extolling the virtues of the West that was published in *The New York Times*. Theodore Roosevelt read it, went West, and bought the Maltese Cross Ranch near the Eatons, and soon the neighbors became friends. Roosevelt later said that the West changed his life, though he was often away from his ranch. The generous and welcoming Eatons were soon hosting hundreds of guests, and the costs were mounting. The guests were happy to pay; initially, the Eatons stuck to the ethics of Western hospitality and refused, but in 1882, Burt Rumsey of New York became the first paying dude.

Larry Larom, a 21-year-old Princeton student, came West on the railroad in 1910. His adventure began as he stepped off the train in the middle of the night at the base of a water tower. His destination was Jim McLaughlin's Valley Home Ranch, on the Shoshone River near Cody. Larom returned five years later with his friend Winthrop Brooks (of the Brooks Brothers clothing company), and they bought the ranch, shortening the name to Valley Ranch. Larom worked hard and learned the skills of ranching and packing. He never lost sight of the East and journeyed there most years, maintaining an office in the Brooks Brothers building in New York. The dudes kept coming.

The Great Northern Railroad was convinced of the value of an organization of dude ranches to maintain standards, promote the concept of ranch vacations, and strengthen their efforts through cooperation. Passenger traffic manager A.B. Smith organized a meeting in Bozeman, Montana, in 1926. There were 70 to 100 ranchers there, and 26 signed up as charter members of the Dude Ranchers' Association. Larry Larom was elected the first president, a position he held for 18 years.

Dude ranching started here at the Custer Trail Ranch near Medora, North Dakota. The ranch was named for the fact that George Armstrong Custer once camped nearby. America's first dude ranchers, the Eaton brothers, came here in 1879, taking over an abandoned stage company cabin. Their arrival was three years after the Battle of Little Bighorn, 10 years before the Dakota Territory became two states, and four years before Medora was named by the Marquis de Mores for his wife, Medora von Hoffman. In 1882, Burt Rumsey became the first dude when he signed the ranch guest book and paid $10 per week. (Courtesy of the Dude Ranch Foundation.)

Howard Eaton, who was from Pittsburgh, first came west to Omaha, Nebraska, when he was 17 years old in 1868. He returned home and did some traveling, including a few months at sea with his brother Charles. Howard permanently returned to the Dakota Territory in 1879. Brother Alden moved west in 1881, and Willis joined them in 1882. Seen here from left to right are Alden, Howard, and Willis Eaton. (Courtesy of Eatons' Ranch.)

In 1882, the Eatons convinced A.C. Huidekoper, from a prominent Dutch family and whom they knew from Pennsylvania, to partner with them. The Custer Trail Cattle Company was formed, and cattle and horse raising began. (Courtesy of Eatons' Ranch.)

A bronc is being saddled in a chute in this photograph. Horses were essential to ranch work, and breaking and training them was an ongoing part of a ranch. When Howard Eaton first moved to the Badlands area of the Dakota Territory, he and a partner, E.G. Paddock, made money returning lost horses to railway camps. They also sold the railway men meat from the buffalo, elk, deer, sheep, bear, and antelope that they hunted. (Courtesy of Eatons' Ranch.)

The winter of 1886–1887 was brutal, and there were devastating cattle die-offs. Once through the winter, the Custer Trail Cattle Company found that its losses took it back to its original herd numbers. Huidekoper was disillusioned and amicably left the partnership to concentrate on raising horses, which had fared the deadly weather better. (Courtesy of Eatons' Ranch.)

Howard Eaton accidentally changed American history when an enthusiastic letter he wrote to a friend about the West was published in a New York newspaper. Theodore Roosevelt read it and came to North Dakota in 1893. Soon he had his own ranch, the Maltese Cross, near the Eatons. This is a wide view of the ranch the Eatons built in Wyoming. (Courtesy of Eatons' Ranch.)

Riding a horse into the mountains for a meal has always been a highlight at dude ranches. From 1882, when Burt Rumsey became the first paying guest, until 1887–1888, the Eatons hosted dudes who paid and those who did not. For one of those years, the Eatons counted 2,200 free guest meals. (Courtesy of Eatons' Ranch.)

Horses from Eatons' Ranch are seen in the forest in this photograph. Following the cattle losses of 1887–1888, the Eatons decided to charge $10 per week for each guest. Still the dudes came. By 1891, dudes were a regular and important part of the ranch during the summer. (Courtesy of Eatons' Ranch.)

Howard Eaton is at the head of this mountain trail ride at Eatons' Ranch. In 1898, Howard led his first pack trip into Yellowstone National Park with 40 dudes, all men. Pack trips are large, complex operations with riding horses and pack animals, equipment, and supplies for all the dudes and staff. Howard led a pack trip to Yellowstone every year after that. (Courtesy of Eatons' Ranch.)

An Eatons' Ranch pack string and cabin are seen here. Pack trips were a popular and important part of early dude ranching. They took dudes to places that would be nearly impossible to experience otherwise. In 1902, the Eatons allowed women to join their annual Yellowstone trip for the first time. Yellowstone, founded in 1872, was the only national park that predated dude ranching. (Courtesy of Eatons' Ranch.)

A guest looks down at Eatons' Ranch. Around the turn of the 20th century, thousands of dry farmers were moving into the Badlands, taking over rangeland and pushing ranchers out. At the same time, the Eatons' guests were pulling them west, asking for pack trips into Yellowstone and the Big Horn Mountains. (Courtesy of Eatons' Ranch.)

Guests are pictured on horses waiting to head out on a ride. In 1903, the Eatons accepted a cash offer for Custer Trail Ranch. Now they had the opportunity to find the perfect location for a dude ranch. The family knew what they were looking for: great riding with mountains and level ground at an elevation that was high enough for great summers and low enough for tolerable winters. (Courtesy of Eatons' Ranch.)

Some of the cabins at Eatons' Ranch are shown here. The family had not planned to open in 1904, as the ranch, including cabins, had to be built. Seventy guests came anyway and slept in tents or on the ground, ate meals on ironing boards, and helped clean the cabins as the builders finished them. (Courtesy of Eatons' Ranch.)

Pictured here are the main buildings of Eatons' Ranch. The big move from the Custer Trail Ranch to the new Eatons' Ranch came in 1904. A brochure describing the new ranch was mailed out to its guest list. (Courtesy of Eatons' Ranch.)

This is another great view of Eatons' Ranch. In 1905, the Eatons campaigned for a railroad stop at the ranch. In 1910, Burlington Northern granted it. The family was also successful in getting a post office located on the ranch with the official address of Wolf, Wyoming. (Courtesy of Eatons' Ranch.)

From left to right, Alden, Willis, and Howard Eaton are shown at their new ranch in Wyoming. Once settled in, the three brothers were the first to sign the guest register, Howard as "Ever Genial," Willis as "Best Ever," and Alden as "Cheer Up," and they also signed as Beau Brummell. (Courtesy of Eatons' Ranch.)

An Eatons' Ranch hunting pack string is shown here. Howard Eaton remained active throughout his life. Struthers Burt of the Bar BC Ranch ran into Howard on the top of the Continental Divide in 1922, the year Howard died at 71. He had just finished up a three-week hunting trip when they met. Struther's description of Howard was "A big burly gray man, with absent-minded eyes that missed nothing and could be sharp as knives and with a bad limp in one leg. Half the bones in his body had been broken in falls from horses and by other accidents, yet he walked faster than any man I have ever seen." (Courtesy of Eatons' Ranch.)

The Eatons' Ranch swimming pool is shown in the early days. Though the family has always believed in the importance of comfortable accommodations and great food and activities in addition to the central experience of riding, they have never lost sight of the importance of remaining an authentic working cattle ranch. This remains true to this day. (Courtesy of Eatons' Ranch.)

A cowboy named Curley is riding a bronc with a big audience of dudes at Eatons' Ranch. For five generations, the family has lived and worked on the ranch as real cowboys and cowgirls. Throughout the years, they have not depended on others for the skills and knowledge necessary to run a ranch, they have passed them down through the family. (Courtesy of Eatons' Ranch.)

This photograph shows horses and riders from Eatons' Ranch in Glacier National Park. Howard Eaton began annual pack trips through Glacier in 1915. These were less luxurious than the Yellowstone trips. Artist Charley Russell was a guest, as was Mary Roberts Rinehart, who wrote a book about her experience, *Through Glacier Park, Seeing America First with Howard Eaton.* (Courtesy of Eatons' Ranch.)

Mary Roberts Rinehart was a frequent guest at Eatons' Ranch. This was her cabin. Rinehart was one of the first US correspondents to report on World War I. She was also taken by the West and often endured great hardship to see it. Most of what she wrote supported preservation of the West. *Lost Ecstasy* was about Eastern girls coming out West and meeting cowboys. *Sleeping Giant* was aimed at explaining and gathering support for national parks. (Courtesy of Eatons' Ranch.)

Eatons' Ranch horses are saddled and ready for the next trail ride. Jeff Way, the general manager today, is the fifth generation of the Eaton family. According to Frank Eaton, there have been guest families with seven generations who have stayed at the ranch. The ranch has also hosted a long list of celebrities, including Cary Grant, Will Rogers, Hans Kleiber, Charles Russell, and Will James. (Courtesy of Eatons' Ranch.)

This photograph is titled "Working the Cavvy." Horses are a big draw to ranches, but as Mary Roberts Rinehart said, the ranch vacation could be for the whole family; they could work with the cowboys, ride, read, or fish. Rinehart also told of the relaxing atmosphere of the West, including how Eatons' Ranch guests would leave their old ranch clothes at the ranch and put them back on as soon as they returned. (Courtesy of Eatons' Ranch.)

Big Bill Eaton, who was known for his impressive rope tricks, ran the family ranch along with his father, Alden, and later with his wife, Patty. As Bill got older, his daughter Nancy and her husband, Tom Ferguson, took over. Following Tom's death in 1983, Frank Eaton and Tom's son Bill Ferguson and wife, Karen, ran the ranch. (Both, courtesy of Eatons' Ranch.)

From left to right are Alden, Big Bill, and Willis Eaton. Neither Howard nor Willis ever married or had children. Alden and son Bill kept the family line going. Howard died in 1922 of appendicitis, and Willis died in 1929 of a heart attack. Alden died at the ranch in 1937. While Howard was undoubtedly the most famous of the brothers, Willis and Alden worked hard and were instrumental in the success of the ranch. (Courtesy of Eatons' Ranch.)

Riders on Roosevelt Trail are shown here. The Eatons were always recognized for their dedicated and special brand of Western hospitality. Their concern for and interest in their guests was unwavering. Still, their friendship and association with Theodore Roosevelt was helpful. Roosevelt was president at the time of the Eatons' move to Wyoming. (Courtesy of Eatons' Ranch.)

Howard Eaton Trail in Yellowstone National Park continues as a memorial to the many contributions he made to the park and the West. In 1902, Howard bought 18 bison from Charles Allard's estate. Later that year, he sold them to Yellowstone, where they mixed with three from Charles and Mary Goodnight. That herd is often credited with saving bison from extinction. While that may be an exaggeration, this herd was critical to the return of bison to Yellowstone. (Courtesy of Eatons' Ranch.)

The Eatons' Ranch herd ("cavvy") is seen above. A group of riders from Eatons' Ranch is seen in front of the Glacier Park Hotel below. A later Wyoming dude rancher believed that dude ranching would not have developed as it did without the Eatons' ideas and perceptiveness. People's desire to visit the West would have been inadequately met by hotels and boardinghouses. (Both, courtesy of Eatons' Ranch.)

Irving Hastings "Larry" Larom fell in love with the West in 1910 after attending several of Buffalo Bill's exhibitions in Madison Square Garden with his father. He became acquainted with Bill himself and was inspired to travel to Cody, Wyoming. He stayed three summers with Jim and Jennie McLaughlin at Valley Home Ranch, loving the outdoor life, and in 1913, aged 24, he decided he wanted to be a dude rancher. A well-educated, affluent Easterner, Larom knew nothing about dude ranching, but he believed that this beautiful, natural area on the South Fork of the Shoshone River would provide the perfect escape for wealthy, elite guests from the East. The outbreak of World War I in 1914 virtually closed the European continent to American visitors, who began looking west for their summer breaks. With the support of his wealthy father and asking his friend Winthrop Brooks to be his partner, he made an offer on the ranch. (Courtesy of American Heritage Center, University of Wyoming.)

In June 1915, Larom and Winthrop Brooks (heir to Brooks Brothers) secured the ownership of the renamed Valley Ranch. Charging $90 per month, they attracted wealthy Eastern guests bored with city life who could afford expensive, extended vacations in what they saw as the "sanctuary" of the West. The picture below of Larom (center) and four other men captures the Eastern style of early guests. (Both, courtesy of American Heritage Center, University of Wyoming.)

This photograph shows Larom posing with a female guest outside one of the ranch cabins. Although he was from a wealthy background, in 1920, Larom married a Cody girl, Irma Drew, who understood what life on a ranch entailed. He wrote to his friend Brooks in 1923, "The wives of you men in the East wouldn't and couldn't stand it, year after year." Their marriage lasted until his death 53 years later. (Courtesy of American Heritage Center, University of Wyoming.)

The golden years of Valley Ranch were the 1920s, and it was not unusual to have 100 guests or more daily through the summer. The picture above shows a group of women dressed in typical dude apparel. Valley Ranch advised a simple dress code: "Old clothes and the ability to fit into the surroundings are all that are necessary. For the ladies we recommend . . . light weight riding breeches, another of heavier material, flannel shirts, western hat, plain riding boots, bathing suit, saddle slicker, warm stockings, short walking skirt and stout walking shoes." Almost everyone went for a ride in the freshness of the morning. In the afternoon, there was tennis, swimming, and bridge. Dances were held regularly on Saturday nights. Families with children were also welcome on the ranch, and the picture below demonstrates that the kids fully embraced the dress code, too. (Both, courtesy of American Heritage Center, University of Wyoming.)

The 1920s also saw a constant building program for the ranch. This photograph shows some of the cabins built among the cottonwood trees planted by Larom when he first acquired the ranch. Natural springs provided drinking water, and in 1921, Larom built a swimming pool. In 1922, a dining room was added together with an icehouse to store ice cut from the river in winter. (Courtesy of American Heritage Center, University of Wyoming.)

Larom believed in preserving the rustic cabins of the original homestead, as seen in this photograph. Fuel-powered generators were used for lighting and heating water for the bathhouse. It was not until the 1940s that electricity was brought to Valley Ranch. Struthers Burt wrote after visiting in 1932 that Larom had created "Just the right combination of old ranch, clean ranch and beautiful ranch." (Courtesy of American Heritage Center, University of Wyoming.)

Other cabins were slightly more "modern," as seen here. After dinner, guests would return to their cabins to rest, socialize, or play bridge. The Chuck Wagon served soft drinks and food throughout the day, but no liquor was served in the public rooms, so guests served cocktails to their friends in their cabins. The Recreation Room, where the dances were held, was built in 1920 to hold 50 guests. (Courtesy of American Heritage Center, University of Wyoming.)

Pictured here are other buildings and cabins at Valley Ranch. Families, couples, individuals, and children were all welcomed between June and October. Guests had to get along with each other, since the ranch was isolated and many stayed for several weeks. A great sense of community developed along with a loyalty to the ranch that brought them back. (Courtesy of American Heritage Center, University of Wyoming.)

This image of wranglers bringing horses across the Southfork River gives a sense of the spectacular scenery. Ranch workers got up at 5:30 a.m. They breakfasted in their own rooms before leaving for work. While the cooks went to the kitchen, the wranglers crossed the river to drive the horses in. Many guests rose early to watch the stampede as the horses were herded into the corrals. (Courtesy of American Heritage Center, University of Wyoming.)

Larom is seen here with three female guests with the backdrop of the Absaroka Mountains. Visiting the ranch helped Easterners develop an appreciation of the beautiful natural environment of the South Fork. Valley Ranch grew to around 6,000 acres, including owned or leased land and forest permit areas. By 1935, there were over 100 log and frame buildings nestled in the trees housing guests who loved the ranch. (Courtesy of American Heritage Center, University of Wyoming.)

Guests prepare to go out on a ride. Each dude was allocated his or her own horse and was expected to collect its bridle and take it down to the corral to wait while the wrangler got the horse ready. Then the guests mounted. Rides went out twice a day, six days a week. Larom expected punctuality for rides and for meals—breakfast at 7:30 a.m., lunch at 12:30 p.m., and dinner at 6:30 p.m. (Courtesy of American Heritage Center, University of Wyoming.)

A fisherman shows his catch. As well as the activities to occupy the guests, the ranch itself was like a small, self-sufficient city. It had a post office—mail was collected and delivered three times a week—a dairy herd, nearly 300 saddle horses, hundreds of chickens, hogs, and a vegetable garden. Many wild animals also visited the ranch, including deer, elk, bighorn sheep, and troublesome bears. (Courtesy of American Heritage Center, University of Wyoming.)

This image is of a classroom at Valley Ranch. Larom established a school for boys in 1922 to prepare students for the College Entrance Examination Board. Courses offered were English, French, German, Latin, a broad range of mathematics, and US and ancient history. In 1925, the school became an examination center, which was considered a great honor. Classes began at 8:30 a.m. and ended at 2:00 p.m., with half-days Wednesdays and Saturdays. (Courtesy of American Heritage Center, University of Wyoming.)

Larom is pictured with a group of students. Classes were adjusted to meet boys' individual needs. The brochure stated that, as well as academic study, the school offered "Christian" boys the opportunity to experience the Western lifestyle. There was no room for "indifferent, fault-finding boys who were not cheerful or sportsmanlike." The time required to prepare for the examination was four years or less, depending on ability. (Courtesy of American Heritage Center, University of Wyoming.)

Young men prepare for a polo match. After class, the afternoons were time for outdoor activities and sports. Polo was considered a rich man's game and reflected the affluent background of the boys. Rifle practice, trapping, football, and hiking were some of the other activities on offer. Some days, if the weather was good, classes were cancelled and the boys and masters went on an all-day horseback trip. (Courtesy of American Heritage Center, University of Wyoming.)

These two pictures illustrate the wildness of the country and the opportunity it provided for pack trips. Valley Ranch had an excellent and well-equipped pack outfit, including guides, cooks, and wranglers; a string of 30 pack horses was not unusual. There were three main trails leading to big game areas; bear, moose, elk, deer, and antelope were among the animals hunted. Occasionally the trips were for scientific purposes, collecting specimens to be mounted for display in zoos or museums. Grand Teton National Park, created in 1929, was nearby, and the southeast corner of Yellowstone was just 28 miles from the ranch. Hunting pack trips were organized by Valley Ranch each fall until the 1950s. (Both, courtesy of American Heritage Center, University of Wyoming.)

Children were always welcome at Valley Ranch, as these two photographs show. In 1920, Larom began offering pack trips for boys through Yellowstone and Jackson Hole. The superintendent of Yellowstone, Horace Albright, provided an itinerary and maps marking camping grounds and trails that the boys on horseback could take while the equipment wagons advanced by road. Larom chartered a Pullman to transport the boys from New York to Cody. Safety on the trail was a concern. A physician accompanied them, and after two boys had to be rushed home because of a sick relative, Larom had every confidence in the Yellowstone organization's ability to locate a party in an emergency. Each boy paid $650 for the pack trip of 40–45 days and around $200 for the train journey. In 1922, Larom began pack trips for girls too. The trips always travelled separately but would meet at a campsite on the Snake River for a social event. (Both, courtesy of American Heritage Center, University of Wyoming.)

When Larom sold the ranch in 1969, the guest list had over 16,000 names, including Hollywood celebrities like Robert Taylor and Barbara Stanwyck; well-known artists like Levon West, James Kenneth Ralston, and Marie Haughton Spaeth; and sculptors like Madeline Park, Alexander Phimister Proctor, and Gutzon Borglum. All came to enjoy and record the beauty of the surrounding country and wildlife. Larom (left) is pictured with Secretary of the Interior Douglas McKay in the mid-1950s. (Courtesy of American Heritage Center, University of Wyoming.)

These images show Larry Larom in his office and at his gate at Valley Ranch. As dude ranching became big business, it made sense to organize. In 1926, the Dude Ranchers' Association was formed. Larom became its first president. His background, self-confidence, and connections were a great advantage to the association, particularly during the Depression. He also worked tirelessly for the preservation of wildlife, often endangered by hunting. He was involved in the US Forest Service, National Park Service, US Bureau of Fisheries, and Wyoming Game Protective Association and was appointed chair of President Coolidge's Elk Commission. In 1940, Secretary of the Interior Harold Ickes offered him the office of director of the National Park Service, a position he did not accept. Larom's influence on dude ranching and his services to the community and his country are far reaching. Had he not cancelled his trip on the *Titanic* in 1912, it might have been a different story. Valley Ranch closed in 1987. (Both, courtesy of American Heritage Center, University of Wyoming.)

Two

Jackson and the Tetons Area

The Tetons are likely the most dramatic mountain range in the United States, seeming to rise suddenly from the valley around them. They are also one of the youngest ranges in the country. Glaciers also left their mark on the area.

The valley drew mountain men such as David Jackson (for whom the valley is named) as early as 1811. In 1860, mountain man Jim Bridger guided a military mapping expedition into Jackson Hole. In 1870, there was a relatively small gold rush into the area due to false information. Overall, prospectors and miners found little success.

Homesteading in the valley started around 1884, with 639 counted in 1900. The 1920 population had risen to 1,381 residents. The short growing season, harsh winters, and volatile weather overall made Jackson Hole a very tough place to make a living. Many ranches found an opportunity in the tourists heading to Yellowstone. Dude ranches were the next natural step. Nathaniel Burt wrote in *A Classless Society: Dude Ranching in the Tetons, 1908–1955*:

> Dude ranches boasted a classless society full of class, where the swagger of Western horsemen blended on equal terms with the swagger of adventurous, anti-conventional Eastern aristocracy. Everyone—ranchers, Jackson storekeepers, hired hands, dudes—were caught up in this society, involved in the intense feuds and friendships, the bitter causes (park extension and related problems), took sides, cheated on each other selling horses and playing poker, loved, hated, even married each other.

Though dude ranch numbers have declined overall, Jackson and the Tetons area boasts the most operating today.

In 1967, Charles Moore was quoted as saying, "Had it been possible for a boy to choose where and when he was to be born and where he was to spend his boyhood days, I do not think he could have chosen a life more interesting as to time and place. I grew up in fascinating country surrounded by Indians, soldiers, cowboys, hunters, trappers, freighters, stagecoach drivers, and now and then, outlaws." (Courtesy of CM Ranch.)

Charles Moore was born in 1880 and grew up at Fort Washakie on the Shoshone Indian Reservation. He, his mother, and two sisters were sent east to secondary school. After returning west, following working on ranches, time in Chicago, and a stint in Buffalo Bill's Wild West Show, he entered the University of Michigan Law School. After one year of practicing law in Cheyenne, he missed the outdoors and returned to ranching. (Courtesy of CM Ranch.)

The chuck wagon is the outside kitchen for a camp meal at the CM Ranch. The ranch, named for its founder, Charles Moore, began in 1920, when the property near Dubois was purchased and cabins were built. The origins of it all go back to 1895, when Moore began bringing friends from the East where he was in school. He had learned hunting, trapping, and tracking from the Indians and knew the Wind River area well. He took his friends hunting and on pack trips. (Courtesy of CM Ranch.)

A camping party is seen here. Around 1907, Charles Moore began to think of putting together ranch trips for teenage boys through Yellowstone Park. The boys traveled by train to Lander, where they were met by some of the earliest automobiles. The car journey to the ranch took all day on the rough, up-and-down road. The entire trip lasted 10 weeks and cost $250. Soon, the parents wanted to experience the trips also, and the concept for the CM Ranch was born. (Courtesy of CM Ranch.)

A cook works at Charles Moore's Summer Camp for Boys. The camp advertised: "Unlike other camps, we are not confined by the narrow limits of one little lake. Our camping grounds are limited only by the endurance of power and time itself. Summer finds our camp upon the shores of dozens of beautiful mountain lakes and streams, each wandering in and out, and new scenes are countlessly before our wondering eyes. Each day that camp is moved, the wagons are sent ahead to the next camping ground—never far enough to make a tiresome trip, and on horseback, the boys ride here and there with the Director, taking in the interesting sights along the way. This is the land of *The Virginian* and the cowboy is seen in his native state, riding, roping, branding, etc." (Courtesy of CM Ranch.)

The CM Ranch is seen in its current location on Jakey's Fork. It began in the 1920s with a few log cabins, a dining room, and a bathhouse with running water for showers and toilets. The water was heated by coal-burning monkey stoves. With cabins, baths, meals, and horses, the CM Ranch became a dude ranch. (Courtesy of CM Ranch.)

Charles Moore married Marion Laidlaw on May 20, 1927. Marion was a city girl from Minneapolis who was very concerned about her ability to help run the ranch. As with many early dude ranch wives, she deserved more credit than she got. She became a rancher, often riding up onto Whiskey Mountain to check on the cows. (Courtesy of CM Ranch.)

A CM Ranch pack trip is shown here. Taking guests into the wilderness on pack trips was a big part of the operation. In 1930, Charles Moore purchased the Simpson Lake cabins. The cabins were hand-built on site. Furniture and equipment were created from the materials at hand or hauled in. The cabins remained a part of the CM operation until 1997, when the US Forest Service declined to renew the permit. (Courtesy of CM Ranch.)

Les and Alice Shoemaker bought the CM Ranch from Charles and Marion Moore in 1952. Les was a local Forest Service ranger, and Alice and Marion were friends. The Shoemaker family, including Leslie and Barbara (Les and Alice's daughters), Erroll "Pete" Peterson (Leslie's husband) and Lisa Romaine Peterson (Pete's second wife) worked together as owners and operators until 1997, when they sold the ranch. (Courtesy of CM Ranch.)

A man looks across the bridge to the CM Ranch. In 1997, Jay Kemmerer and his sisters, Connie Kemmerer and Betty Gray, bought the ranch they had visited as children. Their commitment to preserving their historic ranch and maintaining its original character continues today. (Courtesy of CM Ranch.)

The Triangle X Ranch is seen here. Utah cattle rancher John S. Turner purchased Bill Jump's homestead property in 1926 after Jump was injured in a horse accident and needed money. When Jump told Turner his asking price, Turner replied that it was worth twice that and then followed through and paid double. (Courtesy of Triangle X Ranch.)

Horses come through the gate at the Triangle X Ranch. In 1926, John S. Turner arrived in Jackson Hole at his new ranch with a family friend and two of his sons, John C. and Burt. In that first short summer, the four men dug a basement for the main lodge. During the winter, they pulled logs out of the forest using teams of horses. They were able to complete their guest cabins, some outlying buildings, and the two-story main lodge, now the main house. Since most buildings in Jackson Hole were short, one-story buildings, the new lodge was an impressive addition to that part of the valley. (Courtesy of Triangle X Ranch.)

Riders at the Triangle X Ranch are seen here. In the spring of 1927, the Turners drove their livestock from Utah to their new ranch in Wyoming. That same first season, the family began hosting guests, making the Triangle X a working dude ranch. John S., known locally as "Dad," and his wife, Maytie, later founded two other dude ranches in the area, now known as Turpin Meadow and Heart 6. (Courtesy of Triangle X Ranch.)

The original kitchen for the Triangle X Ranch is seen here with the Tetons in the background. John C. Turner took the ranch over when his parents and the rest of the family moved on to other ranches. John was known as a hardworking, quiet man with a great wit. He was also an accomplished horseman, hunter, fisherman, and guide. He founded hunting camps and a pack trip operation into the Teton wilderness that is the oldest wilderness outfitting effort run by one family on national forest lands in the United States. (Courtesy of Triangle X Ranch.)

Louise Mapes, the daughter of Harold "Skipper" Mapes and Maria Vazques, takes a moment with one of her horses, Diablo. Louise was born in 1913 in Mexico, where her father worked as a surveyor, engineer, and mine superintendent from 1910 to 1927. Due to the Mexican Revolution, much of this time was dangerous, causing Skipper to send Louise to a convent in San Antonio at five years old. When he could, Skipper would pick Louise up to travel. In 1927, on one of their trips, they found their way to Jackson Hole on the shores of Jenny Lake, and so began a lifetime love of this valley and mountains for Skipper and Louise. (Courtesy of Triangle X Ranch.)

Louise Mapes and her father, Skipper, settled in a cabin near Moose, after which she wanted to find a guide to help her hunt her first elk. Late in the fall, after most outfitters had closed up, the Moose postmaster, Reed Turner, told the Mapeses that his brother John C. at the Triangle X might still be open. Louise and Skipper drove the 12 miles to the ranch, where John reluctantly agreed to guide Louise. Despite the winter weather, Louise kept up with John and bagged a six-point bull. (Courtesy of Triangle X Ranch.)

John C. Turner is at center with Louise and their son Harold below him and Skipper at right (the person at left is unidentified), with fish caught for dinner. John and Louise were married in 1935, at the same time "Dad" and the rest of the family moved to Turpin Meadow, taking much of the livestock and equipment. John and Louise were left with $90 in the bank and only a few cattle and horses. The newlyweds took the challenge, determined to expand the rolls of guests and to grow the livestock herd. (Courtesy of Triangle X Ranch.)

Louise Turner stands in front of the ranch station wagon with sons Harold (left) and Johnny. Most successful dude ranches had strong matriarchs. She was the consummate hostess for the guests and a demanding leader of the staff. Louise was attractive, stylish, gregarious, and welcoming. (Courtesy of Triangle X Ranch.)

Louise Turner skis behind the Triangle X Ranch cabins. She sadly lost her husband, John, in 1960. She later married Robert S. Bertschy, a decorated World War II Navy captain. Bob was an excellent fly fisherman who guided guests on the Snake River. He was also known for being able to fix almost anything on the ranch. (Courtesy of Triangle X Ranch.)

John Turner built an innovative saw for firewood mounted on a sled with a truck engine and a three-foot-diameter blade. It cut wood fast but was dangerous. Cutting wood was critical, because for more than 25 years, the ranch operated solely on wood for heating and cooking. Rural electric power was not available at the Triangle X until 1953. (Courtesy of Triangle X Ranch.)

At the Triangle X Ranch, the Turner family cut blocks of ice from beaver ponds and hauled them back to the ranch on sleighs. The ice blocks were then packed in sawdust to preserve them. The ice was used to refrigerate food during the spring, summer, and fall. (Courtesy of Triangle X Ranch.)

Putting up hay is essential for ranches like Triangle X. From November until May, each horse, mule, or cow will eat about two tons of hay. With about 250 horses and mules, the need for hay was huge. Preparing and irrigating the land, protecting the crops, and stacking the hay was a big effort. At the Triangle X, the guests often pitched in to help. (Courtesy of Triangle X Ranch.)

The Turners were great hosts and expert ranchers, and many of their guests came back over and over because of them. This is a great view of the other draws the Triangle X had: horses and one of the best views of the Tetons in the valley. (Courtesy of Triangle X Ranch.)

Louise Turner had a unique and efficient way of getting young Harold and herself around the Triangle X ranch in the winter. (Courtesy of Triangle X Ranch.)

As Grand Teton National Park expanded, it acquired homesteads and ranches. The park generally destroyed the historic structures that came with the property. The Turners preserved many of these buildings by moving them to the Triangle X Ranch. The ranch barn, a log schoolhouse, a roadside inn, buildings from the town of Moran, and the original Gros Ventre post office are all now part of the ranch. (Courtesy of Triangle X Ranch.)

To accommodate World War I veteran pilots who came to the ranch to hunt and fish, the Triangle X Ranch built one of Jackson's first airstrips. Teams of horses cleared the strip directly above the ranch buildings. Pilots buzzed the ranch to call for the buckboard to transport them to the ranch. (Courtesy of Triangle X Ranch.)

In the early years at the Triangle X Ranch, trips to town meant a two-day covered sleigh ride to Jackson. In the 1940s and 1950s, the Turners took a four- to five-hour sleigh ride to Moose, where they shoveled a ranch vehicle out of the snow and then started it with a small fire under the engine. (Both, courtesy of Triangle X Ranch.)

A long pack string is shown at the Triangle X Ranch. The Turner family established wilderness and game hunting camps in the 1930s and 1940s. Hunters came from all over the world. (Courtesy of Triangle X Ranch.)

Triangle X Ranch riders are seen with the Tetons in the background. Early on, John S. Turner sold the Triangle X Ranch to John D. Rockefeller, who intended for the property to be included in the 1950 expansion of Grand Teton National Park. Today, the Turners proudly operate the last dude ranch concession in the national park system. (Courtesy of Triangle X Ranch.)

The Triangle X is a working ranch where raising, breaking, and branding livestock is a continuous effort. Five generations of the Turner family have owned and operated the ranch, doing the day-to-day work that maintains the Triangle X authenticity and quality. (Both, courtesy of Triangle X Ranch.)

Snow has piled all the way up to the roof of a Triangle X Ranch building above. Skiing often was one of the best ways of getting around in the Jackson-area winters. It was also a great way to have fun. Skijoring was, and is, a popular winter activity in the mountains. The skiers are pulled by horses through the snow, as shown below. (Both, courtesy of Triangle X Ranch.)

Harold, oldest of the third generation of Turners at the Triangle X, is seen here on snowshoes. Harold was president of the Dude Ranchers' Association and a long-serving board member of America Outdoors. John F. served in the Wyoming legislature and as director of the US Fish and Wildlife Service. Donald kept the ranch running and welcomed guests as Turners before him had. Five generations of Turners are dude ranchers who have impacted the land, their guests, and the West. (Courtesy of Triangle X Ranch.)

The land in the Bridger-Teton National Forest, which eventually became Red Rock Ranch, operated now by the MacKenzie family, was settled in the late 1800s by a series of pioneers. Maurice "Shorty" Williams, Jesse Buchanan, and Fred Koerner are listed, but little is known about them. Pictured here is Jesse Buchanan (left) in an image that clearly captures the harsh conditions survived by these early settlers. (Courtesy of Red Rock Ranch.)

Only one early homesteader, James S. Simpson, pictured at left, has left more than a name. He knew the hunting business inside out, and in 1918 provided an outfitting service for wealthy Easterners in search of adventure. His knowledge led to his appointment to the first Wyoming game and fish commission. (Courtesy of Red Rock Ranch.)

The first owner of Red Rock Ranch was Bill Redmond, seen at right with an impressive stack of antlers. Born in Rhode Island in 1878, Redmond was a well-educated man. He became a cattleman after moving west and homesteaded on Spring Gulch near Jackson Hole, eventually becoming the first commissioner and chairman of the board of Teton County. According to John B. Coleman in *Hunting Big Game in Jackson Hole, Wyoming*, he was an impressive man who could "size up an elk quicker than you can see him," described as weighing 225 pounds with a "heart as big as all outdoors." In 1899, he married Ida Simpson (below), sister of Jim Simpson, and bought the land that became Red Rock Ranch from Jim in 1916. Bill and Ida had three children: Larry, Gertrude, and Dorothy. (Both, courtesy of Red Rock Ranch.)

The photograph above is of the Redmond house, built in 1918 by Henry Crabtree. Until then, the family lived in tents, braving all weather including floods. Bill sold the ranch sight unseen to a wealthy Washington businessman, Eugene Meyer, in 1929. Meyer had always wanted to own a ranch. According to his daughter Ruth Meyer Epstein, "One night he went to a dinner party and ended up with a ranch and a red Irish Setter." Possession, it seems, was enough; he only visited the ranch twice during his 13 years of ownership. Bill and Ida Redmond continued to manage the ranch for two years after they sold it. Below, Redmond adjusts a pack saddle. (Both, courtesy of Red Rock Ranch.)

The photograph at right shows Fernie C. Hubbard on horseback. He married Bill and Ida's daughter Dorothy, and the couple returned to the ranch to manage it in 1936. They left in the 1940s and moved to a ranch in Montana. Their daughter Nancy Hubbard Adams is pictured below in 1937, aged three. (Both, courtesy of Red Rock Ranch.)

Meyer's wife, Agnes, enjoyed the solitude of Red Rock Ranch and visited often. She liked to camp some miles away from the ranch in order to write and fish for trout. She did miss some of the luxuries of her Washington life, however, and eventually persuaded her French chef to cook at the ranch while she was there. Her daughter Ruth recalls how she loved her childhood visits to the ranch. She was fascinated by the simplicity of life out West, where a handshake was as good as a contract. These pictures capture some of that simplicity. The photograph above, taken around the 1920s by Bill Redmond, shows the lodge and guest cabins. At left, dudes enjoy time on the creek—a far cry from the streets of Washington, DC. (Both, courtesy of Red Rock Ranch.)

In 1943, Eugene Meyer decided to sell the ranch. The new owner was Maj. C.C. Mosley, an experienced pioneer aviator who served in World War I and who trained more than 25,000 pilots at Air Corps schools. By the early 1970s, Mosley's health was deteriorating. He wanted to make sure that the ranch passed on to people who would continue ranching and caring for the land. He found these in the current owners, David and Deborah MacKenzie, who continue to preserve the traditions of dude ranching, providing serenity and adventure for those whose imaginations are still captured by the West. (Courtesy of Red Rock Ranch.)

The entrance to the corrals is shown with the guest cabins and horses in the background. Bar BC was the second dude ranch to open in Jackson Hole, but it quickly became the biggest and the most well-known. Struthers Burt, the owner and a Princeton graduate, had ties to the wealthiest families in Philadelphia. Prices were high, and references were required. (Courtesy of the Jackson Hole Historical Society and Museum.)

This is the main cabin at the Bar BC Ranch. In 1911, Maxwell Struthers Burt and Dr. Horace Carncross formed a partnership while working together at the JY Ranch. They decided to start their own dude ranch and purchased land just west of the Snake River in hopes that the river winds would keep away the mosquitos. (Courtesy of the Jackson Hole Historical Society and Museum.)

The Bar BC Ranch is pictured with the Tetons in the background reflected in the swimming pond. (Courtesy of the Jackson Hole Historical Society and Museum.)

Tony Grace is in a Model T in front of the Jenny Lake Lodge main building, which was constructed from the remains of the Danny Ranch buildings. On June 3, 1922, Tony Grace filed a homestead claim just north of Jenny Lake on the east shore of String Lake. He created his own small, secluded guest ranch with the knowledge he gained working for two of the most successful ranches in the valley at the time. (Courtesy of the Jackson Hole Historical Society and Museum.)

Tony Grace thought of his clients as guests and treated them as equals. They enjoyed participating in the ranch chores, and thanks to their enthusiasm, he had no trouble finding volunteers for work. Tony was active in all ranch activities, always creating an inclusive, family-like atmosphere. The Danny Ranch was one of the shortest lived but also one of the most successful guest ranches in the valley. Hiking, mountain climbing, pack trips, fishing, and swimming were offered. Here guests are mounted up and headed out for a morning ride. Many stayed for two to three weeks, arriving by train to Idaho, where Tony would meet them to transport them to the ranch in wagons over Teton Pass and along the rough local roads. (Courtesy of the Jackson Hole Historical Society and Museum.)

Dudes are out for a ride at the Double Diamond Ranch. Joseph S. Clark Jr., a future senator from Pennsylvania and mayor of Philadelphia, and Frank R. Williams, a wilderness guide, met in 1923 on a pack trip and decided to open a dude ranch specifically for high school and college boys to avoid competing with the existing ranches. (Courtesy of the Jackson Hole Historical Society and Museum.)

A dude cabin at the Double Diamond is shown here. In the spring of 1924, there were a main lodge and 12 small cabins, and 19 boys enrolled from the East. The ranch enjoyed a high success rate, with the Westerner providing the labor and experience while the Easterner provided the funds and clientele. The ranch later transitioned to hosting families and closed after Frank Williams's death in 1964. (Courtesy of the Jackson Hole Historical Society and Museum.)

Pack trips were an extremely popular activity for the boys at the Double Diamond Ranch due to Frank Williams's wilderness experience and vast knowledge. (Courtesy of the Jackson Hole Historical Society and Museum.)

In 1926, Californian Chester Goss had amassed 423 acres just outside of Jackson for what would become the most nontraditional dude ranch of the era, the Elbo Ranch. Local ranchers were outraged by the Elbo's imposing billboard boasting "Home of the Hollywood Cowboy." The ranch only operated for three years before Goss jumped at the opportunity to sell it to the Snake River Land Company. (Courtesy of the Jackson Hole Historical Society and Museum.)

The overflowing stands are testament to the popularity of this nontraditional dude ranch with a stunning backdrop of the Teton Mountains. Elbo Ranch had a store, gas station, rodeo ground, racetrack, baseball diamond, and concessions. There were small cabins and cottages available by the night with running hot water, showers, bathtubs, and electricity. (Courtesy of the Jackson Hole Historical Society and Museum.)

Louis Joy, pictured on his favorite horse, established the JY Ranch in 1908, making it the first dude ranch in Jackson Hole. (Courtesy of the Jackson Hole Historical Society and Museum.)

Louis Joy's wife, Jane, is pictured at Phelps Lake with their Irish setters. The first five guests were Maxwell Struthers Burt from Princeton University and four of his wealthy friends. Between Burt's connections and Joy's ranching skills, they quickly realized they could create the perfect partnership. In 1911, frustrated and feeling used for his social contacts, Burt split from Louis Joy with the intention of starting his own ranch. In 1932, the JY became the private property of the John D. Rockefeller family, who later donated the land to Grand Teton National Park. (Courtesy of the Jackson Hole Historical Society and Museum.)

In 1927, Eva Sanford became one of the last people to file for a homestead on Spread Creek. She had come to the valley as the new schoolteacher. She married her neighbor Fred Topping, and in the fall of 1928, Fred built them a small cabin. Pictured here are two guests of Moosehead Ranch dressed in their finest fishing apparel with their catch from Spread Creek. (Courtesy of the author.)

A trail ride is leaving Moosehead Ranch. Fred's reputation as a hunting guide created a loyal following. He wanted to offer hunters tents on their land, but the weather was too harsh, so he added a kitchen and dining room to their cabin and a guest cabin. As demand increased, they added more cabins. (Courtesy of the Jackson Hole Historical Society and Museum.)

Fred and Eva opened Moosehead Ranch in 1937. For $35 a week, guests could enjoy the main lodge dining room and lounge as well as fresh dairy and vegetables. Horseback riding, hiking, fishing, and hunting trips were offered, and soon they could host 40 guests. In 1967, the Toppings sold the ranch to John Mettler, whose family still owns and operates it. (Courtesy of the Jackson Hole Historical Society and Museum.)

Guests are pictured in front of main lodge of Moosehead Ranch and the Elk Post Office, with a ranch horse grazing in the foreground. (Courtesy of the Jackson Hole Historical Society and Museum.)

The Elk Post Office was moved to Moosehead Ranch when Eva became postmistress. (Courtesy of the Jackson Hole Historical Society and Museum.)

R Lazy S opened in 1948 and appeared a year later in *Dude Ranches Out West*, a travel booklet by the Union Pacific Railroad encouraging Easterners to see the West. Perhaps most notable at the time was that the McConaughy family added electricity and plumbing with hot water. Most dude ranches did not provide modern amenities, believing that part of the appeal of a Western vacation was the rustic accommodations. Ranch guests traveling by wagon to the Church of Transfiguration in Grand Teton National Park are pictured above. Below, longtime wrangler Dan Mortensen gets ready for a trip into the mountains. (Both, courtesy of R Lazy S Ranch.)

The main cabin at the White Grass Ranch is pictured here. (Courtesy of the Jackson Hole Historical Society and Museum.)

This is the White Grass Ranch barn. No less than 12 dude ranches can trace their origins to a stay at the Bar BC, and White Grass was the first. Harold Hammond and George Tucker Bispham met while working at the Bar BC and opened the White Grass in 1919. It was the third dude ranch in Jackson Hole, hosting 10 people in three cabins and a tent. The ranch was passed down within the Hammond family until it closed in 1985. (Courtesy of the Jackson Hole Historical Society and Museum.)

Three

The Yellowstone Area

Yellowstone, the world's first national park, was established in 1872. With almost 3,500 square miles, it is about two-thirds the size of Connecticut. The park lies on a plateau about 8,000 feet above sea level over the Yellowstone Caldera, the largest supervolcano on the continent. An active volcano, it includes half the world's geysers and hydrothermal features. Yellowstone was named a UNESCO World Heritage Site in 1978.

Yellowstone National Park has always had a significant role in dude ranching. Tourists came to see and experience the unique geology, spectacular natural beauty, and diverse and plentiful wildlife. Early ranchers such as the Eatons led pack trips into the park. They were major productions and very popular. Sometimes these park trips led to the organizers building permanent lodgings and starting dude ranches. Having a ranch near the park was very good for business, which is just as true today.

Dewey DeWitt and Lee (Elizabeth) Dominick purchased and started the 7D Ranch in 1958. It had been Dewey's dream to have his own dude ranch in Wyoming since he was a boy visiting in the 1920s. They came up with the name and the brand 7D because of the seven Dominicks that made up Dewey's family: Dewey, Lee, David, Mary, John, Marshall, and Steve. (Courtesy of the 7D Ranch.)

All seven of the Dominicks played active roles in the ranch through the late 1970s. John and Lynn Dominick and their two young sons, Spencer and Stuart, took over managing the ranch until 1981, when Dewey retired from his medical practice and wanted to take over again. Dewey died unexpectedly in May 1982 while driving up to his beloved 7D Ranch. (Courtesy of the 7D Ranch.)

The 7D Ranch's spectacular backdrop drew Marlboro to film there. As one of the most iconic brands, Marlboro demands the best in location and complete authenticity. It found both at the 7D Ranch. (Both, courtesy of the 7D Ranch.)

The Holm Lodge, in Park County, Wyoming, was the first to operate solely as a dude ranch with no working cattle. It was built in 1898 by Aron "Tex" Holm on the north fork of the Shoshone River as an overnight stop for tourists he was taking on camping trips in Yellowstone National Park. It burned in 1914. James William "Billy" Howell, a Cody pioneer and homesteader, bought what remained of the Holm Lodge in 1914 and rebuilt it. Howell enjoyed a 35-year career as a dude rancher and customized his cabins for the families that returned every year. One Eastern couple spent 30 consecutive summers at the Holm Lodge. Howell sold the property in 1947 and retired. The new owners named the ranch Crossed Sabres, based on Howell's brand, and it is still operated as a guest ranch today. Tex Holm's stagecoach is seen in Cody above, and Tex is waiting for a dude party in Cody below. (Both, courtesy of the Jackson Hole Heritage Society and Museum.)

Four

Sheridan and the Big Horns

Sheridan is located halfway between Yellowstone and Mount Rushmore and was where several battles took place between the US cavalry and the Sioux, Cheyenne, Arapaho, Shoshone, and Crow Indian tribes between the 1860s and 1870s. The townsite was surveyed in 1882 by order of John Loucks, the first mayor. He served under Civil War general Phil Sheridan, for whom the town was named.

Chicago investors opened several coal mines along the Tongue River in the 1890s. The mining, along with the Burlington & Missouri Railroad coming to town, sparked growth and a building boom. Agriculture was also a big draw as Midwest farmers settled in the area.

Tourism has a long history in the area with numerous dude ranches, including the original Eatons' Ranch.

Norman Meldrum, the founder of Paradise Ranch, was one of the early cattlemen to settle near the Bighorn Mountains once the Sioux, Cheyenne, and Arapaho Indians had been driven out. Meldrum, a Civil War veteran, had had a successful political career in Colorado and served as lieutenant governor from 1887 to 1890. Having completed his political service, he moved to Buffalo in 1897, attracted by the beauty of the area. He built a log cabin on the site, possibly to lay claim to the land, but did not officially gain title to Paradise until 1909. This picture, entitled "The Summer Home," shows the original cabin built by Meldrum as well as several smaller cabins added later to accommodate the ranch's guests. (Courtesy of Paradise Ranch.)

This picture from a brochure, probably from the late 1950s, shows the location of Paradise Ranch within the boundaries of the Bighorn National Forest, 16 miles west of Buffalo. The ranch log cabins were built in a natural clearing below the pine-tree slopes of the mountains on the banks of French Creek, which provided the ranch with a source of water. (Courtesy of Paradise Ranch.)

These Hereford cattle were brought by Norman Meldrum from Colorado. There is no evidence to suggest that he intended to run anything other than a cattle operation, but things changed in 1902 when his son Gordon, a trained doctor, visited en route from serving as a medic in the Spanish-American War in the Philippines. Gordon could see the potential of a guest ranch and decided to stay. He began ranching with his father and started a medical practice in Buffalo. (Courtesy of Paradise Ranch.)

This photograph, entitled "A Quiet Moment," demonstrates the beauty of the surroundings. It was this and tales of the exciting and dangerous Wild West that attracted people to the area. According to the Meldrum family, newly arrived guests would exclaim "This is just paradise," and the name stuck. Between 1902 and 1907, the Meldrums took in guests from Buffalo and beyond. (Courtesy of Paradise Ranch.)

In 1906, Gordon Meldrum married Mabel E. Lee. She has been described by Mary Humstone and Jessie Nunn in *100 Years of Paradise* as having "endless energy, charisma and strength" and a "love of the outdoors," which made her an ideal partner. Her brothers became wranglers on the ranch. After Gordon's untimely death in 1911, she took over the running of the ranch and built Paradise into one of the major dude ranches in Wyoming. (Courtesy of Paradise Ranch.)

This early photograph shows how the ranch began to develop. By 1915, there were eight cabins along the hillside and some semi-permanent tents positioned to take in the view of the valley and the corrals. The number of cows slowly declined as the Meldrums built up a herd of horses suitable for trail riding. Some guests liked to travel into the woods, and overnight camps were also built for pack trips. Others preferred to stay closer to the ranch, so shorter hikes and rides were also provided. (Courtesy of Paradise Ranch.)

PARADISE RANCH

BUFFALO, WYOMING

ACCOMMODATIONS

Comfortable Quarters, Healthful Fare, Good Water, Baths, Etc.

RATES

$2.50..................Per Day

Family rates furnished on application. Saddle Horses and equipment at reasonable rates.

SEASON

June 1st to December 1st, inclusive

All arrangements by letter or telegram in advance should be addressed to

M. L. MELDRUM,
Buffalo, Wyoming

At first, Paradise Ranch brought in guests by word-of-mouth advertising, but as more and more dude ranches grew up in the area around the Bighorns, it was necessary to produce a brochure to attract guests from further afield. This one is from the early days. As with many of the dude ranches, guests had to produce references, preferably from previous guests, to ensure their suitability. (Courtesy of Paradise Ranch.)

Guests were attracted by the promise of comfort as well as wild nature. A passage from one brochure reads, "Although in the wilds, all the comforts of home are to be had at Paradise Ranch. There are comfortable accommodations for about 40 guests in the modern log cabins. Many of the cabins are heated. . . . Ample bathing facilities with running hot and cold water are provided." Like at other ranches, the guests were given lists of suitable clothing to bring. These pictures of guests from 1915 are special because they show "A Glidden Touring Machine at Paradise." This was the first automobile to cross the Bighorn Mountains. The proud smiles of the people and the dog show how pleased they are with their achievement. (Both, courtesy of Paradise Ranch.)

Mabel, pictured here with her first deer, engaged in all activities on the ranch. She could shoot, ride, hunt, fish, and manage a business with the best of them. Her enjoyment of riding meant that she often led hunting and fishing trips. Her greatest achievement is probably that she successfully ran Paradise for 16 years in a world dominated by men. She finally sold the ranch in 1926 to her friend Frank O. Horton of the nearby HF Bar Dude Ranch. (Courtesy of Paradise Ranch.)

During the golden age of dude ranching in the 1930s and 1940s, Paradise Ranch continued to thrive. As with all dude ranches, guests came for the romance and adventure of the Wild West as well as to escape their normal daily routine. These two pictures show how the emphasis on fun was important to the guest experience. Horseback riding was still the most popular activity. Guests could rely on safe, sure-footed, mountain-bred saddle horses and knowledgeable guides. Long and short trails fit guests' abilities and desires. Fishing was also a popular pastime. Government stocking programs meant that guests were rarely disappointed with the catch. Hunting had been replaced by shooting as an activity, and music was also very important. Guests were also taken on trips into Buffalo or to local dances. (Both, courtesy of Paradise Ranch.)

This photograph illustrates another aspect of guest entertainment reflecting the exotic past of the Bighorn Mountains. (Courtesy of Paradise Ranch.)

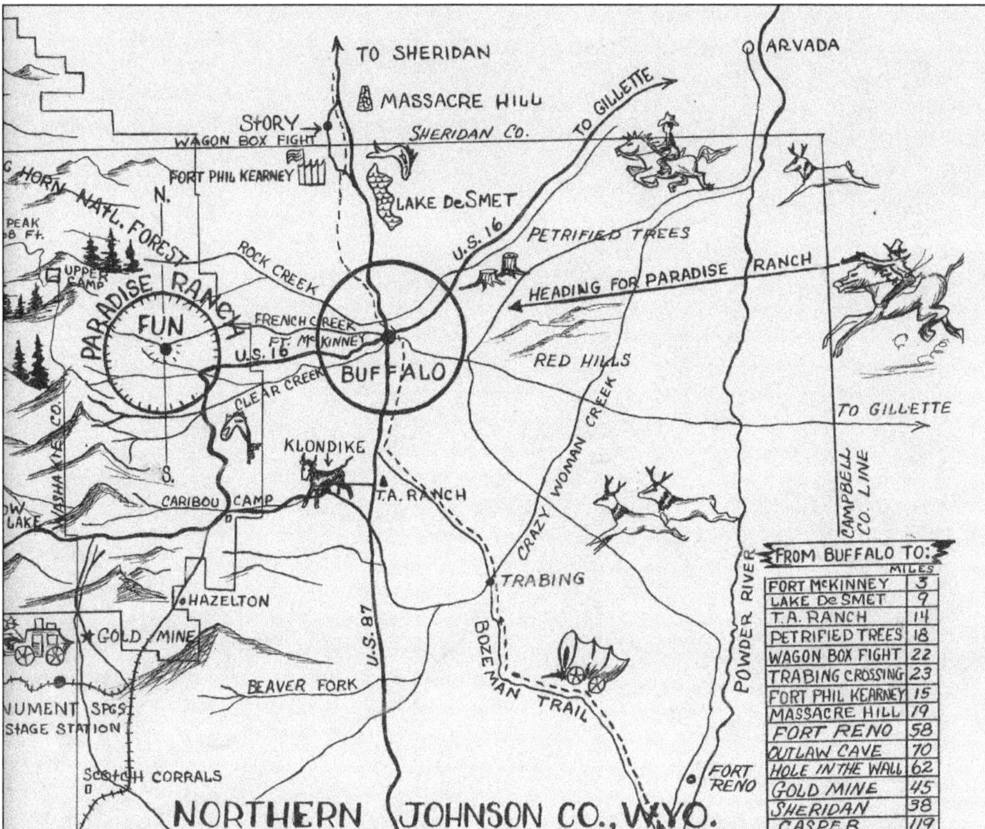

COUNTRY is probably the most interesting and the most beautiful in the entire west. It was the hunting grounds of the Sioux, and Cheyenne Indians. The area is noted for the Custer and Fetterman Massacres, the Wagon Box Fight, the Johnson County Cattle or its Powder River (a mile wide and an inch deep and God only knows how long), and for the fabulously beautiful Hole-in-the-ountry.

See you in the spring!

WRITE SOON—

REFERENCES are required for your protection. We will be glad to send you the names of former guests from your part of the country.

RESERVATIONS must be made in advance, and for a definite period of time. A deposit is required.

RATES and additional information will be sent on request.

ALL HOPE abandon ye who vacation here of ever forgetting Paradise Ranch until you come again!

Your Host
Wyoming Jack O'Brien

This page was taken from a later brochure. The photograph at lower right is of Jack O'Brian, who took over the ranch in 1950. He was a natural showman and had a reputation for being wild. Some of his whiskey-fueled entertainments involved riding a horse into the bar in Buffalo and shooting up the ranch kitchen. Everything was very informal, and there was heavy drinking among the guests and staff. O'Brian's era seemed to be a throwback to the Wild West of legend. Paradise Ranch today continues the traditions, values, and high quality established in the early days. It still flourishes as a popular destination. (Courtesy of Paradise Ranch.)

Staff at HF Bar Ranch use a tractor to move garbage. In the fall of 1910, Warren Gorrell and Frank Horton, brothers-in-law and close friends, first saw the land where they founded HF Bar Ranch in 1911. As an investment banker in Chicago, Warren Gorrell became very wealthy, and his family were the major stockholders in the ranch. (Courtesy of the author.)

The A2Z ranch was part of the Valley Ranch holdings but operated as an entirely separate ranch covering several thousand acres. It offered guests the "Best of Everything" for $56 a week, including a private horse. The living room of the A2Z Ranch is seen here. (Courtesy of the A2Z Ranch.)

This photograph is titled "On the Path from the Corrals." Larry Larom, the owner of Valley Ranch, bought out his partner Winthrop Brooks in 1926. He also added the A2Z Ranch and other ranches owned by Mary Brown Thomas and Juanita Jens. (Courtesy of the A2Z Ranch.)

The lodge building at the Trappers Lodge is shown in 1922. The ranch is located in Shell Canyon, southwest of Sheridan. (Courtesy of the Hideout Lodge and Guest Ranch.)

This is a 1913 photograph of a tent cabin at the Trappers Lodge. These guest accommodations were 12-by-14-foot tents on wooden floors. Two brothers, Gay and Watson Wyman, moved the opposite direction of most dude ranchers, heading east from the Pacific Northwest. They first came in 1906 to visit their sister, who had married a Wyoming rancher. (Courtesy of the Hideout Lodge and Guest Ranch.)

This 1913 photograph shows another view of the main lodge at Trappers Lodge. The Wyman brothers liked Wyoming so much that they brought their $1,600 in savings and in 1908 bought the William Calls homestead. Their parents left Seattle to join their sons at their new cattle ranch. (Courtesy of the Hideout Lodge and Guest Ranch.)

A meal is being prepared outside by the kitchen and housekeeping crew at the Trappers Lodge. Like the Eatons, the Wymans soon had more guests staying longer than they expected or were ready for. As happened at the Eatons', the guests wanted to pay, and the Wymans accepted. (Courtesy of the Hideout Lodge and Guest Ranch.)

Dudes are shown fishing at the Trappers Lodge. When they weren't riding, the guests enjoyed excellent fishing in Trapper and Shell Creeks. Dudes also paid nearly double to stay at the Wymans' enlarged cow camp, which was at an altitude of 8,000 feet. (Courtesy of the Hideout Lodge and Guest Ranch.)

Marina Wister, daughter of Owen Wister (author of *The Virginian*), is in the center of camp at the Trappers Lodge. The Wister family were regular guests who, along with other authors and artists, gave the Trappers Lodge the reputation of being the intellectual dude ranch of the West. (Courtesy of the Hideout Lodge and Guest Ranch.)

Dude William Paton is on horseback at the Trappers Lodge in 1913. He came west from New York for the dry, healthy weather to help with his polio. The wranglers would tie his legs in place so he could ride. William later went on to build the Kedesh Ranch at the mouth of Shell Canyon. (Courtesy of the Hideout Lodge and Guest Ranch.)

Ed Wyman and his wife are picking up guests in Cody for the trip to the Trappers Lodge. Ed Wyman was one of the original board members (1926) of the Dude Ranchers' Association. The Wymans sold the ranch to Brent Wyeth of Wyeth Pharmaceutical of Philadelphia in 1930. The new owners grazed sheep above the lodge, causing water damage and erosion and ultimately forcing the ranch to close. Today, the ranch is owned and operated by the owners of the Hideout Lodge and Guest Ranch. (Courtesy of the Hideout Lodge and Guest Ranch.)

A cowboy stands in the door of the tack room at Spear-O-Wigwam Ranch. Willis Moses Spear, the founder of the ranch, was born in 1862 in Missouri. His parents brought him west to Wyoming Territory in a wagon train when he was 12 years old. Willis and his brother Doc were very successful cattle ranchers, with about three million acres of land and 56,000 cattle at the peak of their business. (Courtesy of Spear-O-Wigwam Ranch.)

Snow covers Spear-O-Wigwam Ranch in a Big Horn Mountain winter. In 1885, Willis Spear married Virginia Belle Benton. They had four children: Jessamine, Willis Benton, Phillip, and Elsa. Jessamine and Elsa were ultimately involved in the dude ranch. All three women in the family—Virginia, Jessamine, and Elsa—were photographers who documented the ranch. (Courtesy of Spear-O-Wigwam Ranch.)

A workman hangs from a crane during construction of the lodge at Spear-O-Wigwam Ranch. The building was in the shape of the ranch's brand, a spear extending from a wigwam. Luke Anderson with Historic Wyoming said, "Spear-O-Wigwam is both architecturally and historically significant. The design of the lodge, especially the spearhead entry, makes the ranch a unique architectural design. Spear-O-Wigwam is an interesting intersection between east and west and between civilization and wilderness." (Courtesy of Spear-O-Wigwam Ranch.)

A log construction crew is working on the Spear-O-Wigwam Ranch lodge. Cattleman and Wyoming state senator (1918–1932) Willis Spear opened his ranch on the Little Goose Creek in Big Horn as a dude operation in 1922, inviting friends from Chicago, Omaha, and other cities. In 1923, Spear took dudes from the ranch in Big Horn to his cow camp in the Big Horn Mountains. That cow camp became a dude ranch and officially opened as Spear-O-Wigwam in 1924. (Courtesy of Spear-O-Wigwam Ranch.)

Cowboys hang around and watch on laundry day with the Spear-O-Wigwam Ranch lodge in the background. Spear's daughter Jessamine took over management of the ranch in 1931. She also managed the family's Montana ranch, the Rosebud X4. This is the period when architect Herschel Elarth designed the extension of the lodge in the shape of a spear. In 1947, the Spear family sold the ranch to Cliff Carroll of Sheridan. (Courtesy of Spear-O-Wigwam Ranch.)

Spear-O-Wigwam's most celebrated guest was Ernest Hemingway, pictured here with trout he caught at the ranch. Hemingway and his wife, Pauline, checked into the ranch on August 19, 1928, and stayed for one week. He completed the first draft for his novel *A Farewell to Arms* during his stay. After his visit, his cabin was renamed Hemingway, which it remains to this day. (Both, courtesy of Spear-O-Wigwam Ranch.)

C. Jack Rhodes Sr., on horseback, is rescuing a Hereford calf in a blizzard on the Pitchfork Ranch. Started as a cattle ranch in 1878 by cattle baron Otto Franc, the Pitchfork Ranch became well known in the 1930s and 1940s for hosting famous people, including Amelia Earhart and Will Rogers. Its notoriety was credited to the photography and promotion of Charles J. Belden, the son-in-law of Franc's partner and investor, Louis Graham Phelps. (Courtesy of Buffalo Bill Center of the West.)

The note on this photograph reads "A herd of 1500 cattle trailing across a blizzard swept range to feed at ranch headquarters." The Pitchfork Ranch also gained recognition for being the location for Marlboro ads, and legend has it that Butch Cassidy stole his first horse from Otto Franc. In 1922, the Pitchfork comprised seven ranches totaling nearly 300,000 acres. The ranch was broken up in the 1940s, but the Belden, Phelps, and Turnell families retained control of over 100,000 acres. (Courtesy of Buffalo Bill Center of the West.)

C. Jack Rhodes Sr. (left) and Hugh Windsor sit at the Pitchfork bunkhouse in the evening playing guitar while a saddled horse waits. Harry Thayer sits inside the bunkhouse. (Courtesy of Buffalo Bill Center of the West.)

From left to right, C. Jack Rhodes Sr., Hughie Windsor, Curly Hollingsworth, Mark Windsor, and Dutch Kreal gamble beside the wagon on the Pitchfork Ranch. A mounted cowboy watches a Hereford herd in the background. The Z-T brand is visible on the wagon, and a Pitchfork branding iron is behind the seated cowboy. (Courtesy of Buffalo Bill Center of the West.)

Four cowboys teach a dude to rope in a corral next to horses and cattle on the Pitchfork Ranch. (Courtesy of Buffalo Bill Center of the West.)

From left to right, Lee Wentworth, C. Jack Rhodes Sr., Mark Windsor, and Shorty Graham (the chore boy) gather near the chuckwagon at night and sing on the Pitchfork Ranch. (Courtesy of Buffalo Bill Center of the West.)

Five

Other Dude Ranch Territory

Wyoming is made for dude ranching. It is the 10th largest state and has the fewest people. The western two-thirds are covered mostly by the Rocky Mountains and rangelands. The eastern third is high-elevation prairie. Almost half of the state is federally owned land, including Grand Teton and Yellowstone National Parks, two national recreation areas, two national monuments, extensive national forests, historic sites, fish hatcheries, and wildlife refuges.

Dudes come for big, beautiful, unspoiled country, recreation, and Western cowboy and ranching culture. Wyoming provides all of that in ways few other places can. Lists of dude ranches from the 1930s, 1940s, and 1950s include 120. While not all ranches are members, there are currently 26 ranches from Wyoming in the Dude Ranchers' Association.

The A Bar A Ranch land has attracted people for centuries, with evidence of Native American settlements in the North Platte River valley long before European settlers arrived in the 1800s. Fur trapping, mining, logging, and ranching opportunities drew settlers, and by the late 1800s, there were many small homesteads and mining claims in the area. This image shows horses pushing hay onto a haystack. (Courtesy of the A Bar A Ranch.)

Along the banks of the North Platte River, in the heart of southern Wyoming's Medicine Bow Mountains, lies the A Bar A Ranch. Established in 1922, it is one of the oldest guest ranches in the country. It is also one of the largest, with nearly 100,000 acres for guests and staff to explore, like those pictured here. (Courtesy of the A Bar A Ranch.)

Andy Anderson and Edward Hubbell, young Princeton graduates, bought the ranch in 1922. They moved west with their wives and named it A Bar H. The guest ranch was immediately successful, but the two wives soon grew incompatible. In 1932, the flip of a silver dollar determined their fates. Anderson won, purchased Hubbell's portion, and renamed the ranch A Bar A. The Charles Gates family of Denver bought the A Bar A in the early 1960s, and it continues to be very successful, entertaining guests of all ages. (Courtesy of the A Bar A Ranch.)

Continually operated as a guest and cattle ranch since 1922, the A Bar A has been home to guests and staff families for multiple generations. (Courtesy of the A Bar A Ranch.)

Medicine Bow Lodge opened as a guest ranch on July 15, 1917. Jessie More and her brother-in-law George "Baldy" Sisson built the lodge to give dudes from the East a place to vacation. Medicine Bow Lodge is located in the Snowy Range in Medicine Bow National Forest, surrounded by old mining and logging towns as well as hundreds of lakes, ponds, and steams. It is currently operated by Tim and Debbie Bishop. (Both, courtesy of Medicine Bow Lodge.)

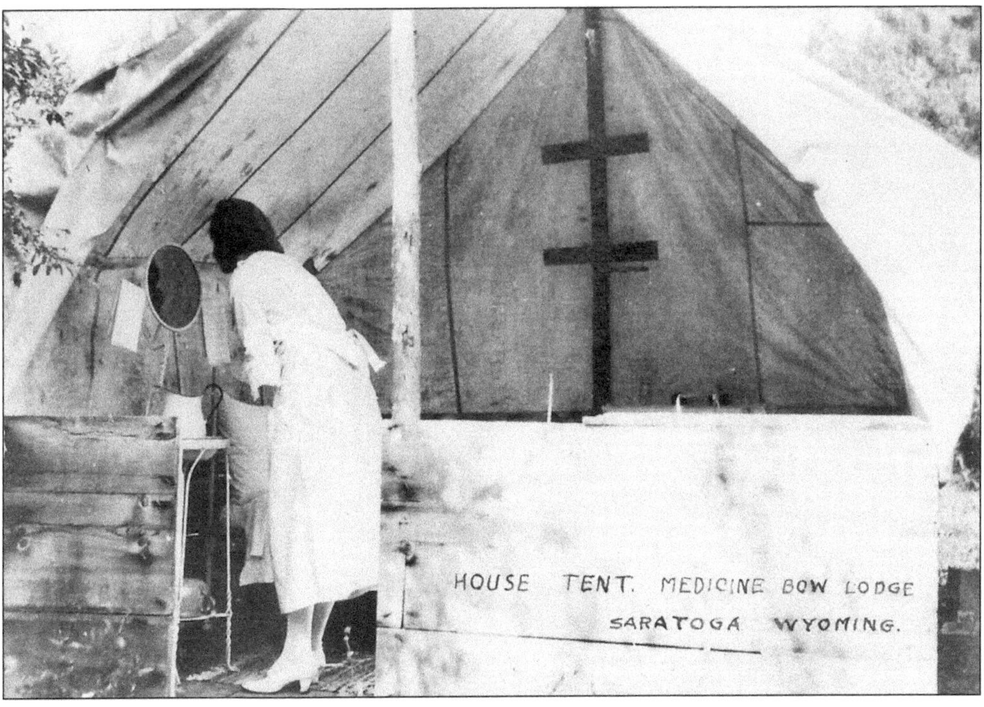

The Vee Bar Ranch lodge was built in 1891 as the home of Lionel C.G. Sartoris, a prominent Wyoming rancher. Sartoris bought the Vee Bar land from homesteader Theodore Brubaker in 1890. Sartoris was English and a partner in the Douglas William Sartoris Cattle Company, which in 1885 was worth an estimated $2 million. By 1892, the company had failed. (Courtesy of Kari Kilmer, manager of the Vee Bar Ranch.)

The Vee Bar Ranch was used as a stagecoach stop and post office and was later bought by Luther Filmore, a Union Pacific Railroad official, and the Wright family, who operated it as a dude ranch in 1912. The five historic buildings include the lodge, original corral, and stock chute. (Courtesy of Kari Kilmer, manager of the Vee Bar Ranch.)

Two fishermen display their catch at the Vee Bar Ranch. The ranch is situated on a bend of the Little Laramie River. The original log lodge was built by the Fillmores in 1901 and expanded in 1911. (Courtesy of Kari Kilmer, manager of the Vee Bar Ranch.)

Irvin "Irv" Lozier is seen in this photograph. His grandparents Irvin M. and Elizabeth "Lizzie" Lozier homesteaded the Box R Ranch in 1900, following earlier visits to the site in 1888. Though beautiful, the land was very difficult ranching country due to the remoteness, high altitude, and short growing season. (Courtesy of the Lozier family.)

Irv Lozier is on the pony with sister Jane (left) and mother Nancy at the Loziers' Box R Ranch. In 1936, Nancy Cook and her father, Benjamin Ladd Cook, from Providence, Rhode Island, were guests at the Z-U Guest Ranch. During several visits, she met the youngest of Irv M. and Lizzie Lozier's four sons, Walter. They married on December 31, 1940, and had three children: Jane (1942), Irv (1945), and Patsy (1947). (Courtesy of the Lozier family.)

Box R Ranch dudes are pictured with fish they have caught. The Loziers' ranch was always a diverse operation, with cattle, dudes, hunting, and fishing. Elizabeth Lozier told her grandson Irv many times in the 1950s and 1960s that the challenges of such a diversified livelihood are a small sacrifice to live in the most beautiful valley in Wyoming. (Courtesy of the Lozier family.)

The Loziers pose with guests at the Box R Ranch. Carl Runguis, a famous wildlife artist, became a close friend to Irv and Lizzie, encouraging and helping them get started in the guest and hunting businesses. (Courtesy of the Lozier family.)

The Lozier family is shown around 1950; from left to right are Walter, Nancy, Irvin, Patsy, and Jane. On New Year's Day 1972, Irv received a call from Solvang, California, police that Walter and Nancy had been killed in a head-on car crash. At 26, Irv was suddenly left to manage the ranch. He continued the hard work of improving and expanding the Box R Ranch as Walt and Nancy had done before him. (Courtesy of the Lozier family.)

Index of Ranches

About the Dude Ranch Foundation

The Dude Ranch Foundation was established in 1988 by Mark Grubbs. He and his wife, Amy, were co-executive directors of the Dude Ranchers' Association and former dude ranch owners.

The original objective was to provide college scholarships to young people who wanted to be involved in dude ranching. In 2003, the vision was expanded to include a museum and heritage center across the street from the Irma Hotel in Cody, Wyoming.

The Dude Ranch Foundation's mission is to protect and preserve the history of dude ranching by maintaining a museum and archives for educating the public on the history of the dude ranching industry. The foundation's Horse Safety Program helps keep both dude ranch guests and our equine friends as safe as possible. Additionally, its mission is to financially assist in the education of persons wishing employment or careers in the dude ranch industry and supporting industries.

Colleen Hodson
Executive Director
The Dude Ranch Foundation (501[c][3])
1122 Twelfth Street
PO Box 2307
Cody, WY 82414
307-587-2339
www.duderanchhistory.org
colleen@duderanch.org

Keeping the Real West Alive

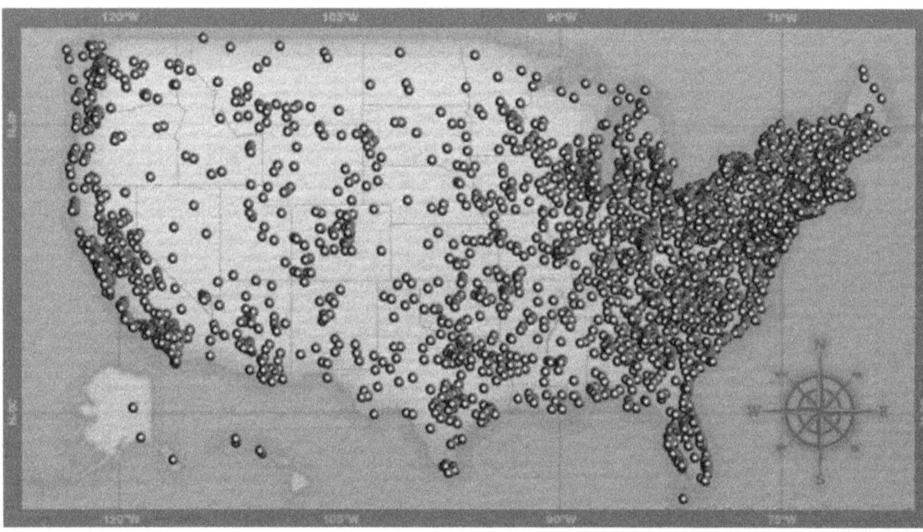

Consistent with our mission to preserve history on a local level, this book was printed in South Carolina on American-made paper and manufactured entirely in the United States. Products carrying the accredited Forest Stewardship Council (FSC) label are printed on 100 percent FSC-certified paper.

MADE IN THE USA

www.ingramcontent.com/pod-product-compliance
Lightning Source LLC
LaVergne TN
LVHW071100050926
847404LV00038B/473
* 9 7 8 1 4 6 7 1 0 3 3 3 6 *